**Cover and Title Page:** Nathan Love

# www.mheonline.com/readingwonders

Send all inquiries to:
McGraw-Hill Education
2 Penn Plaza
New York, NY 10121

ISBN: 978-0-02-131387-7
MHID: 0-02-131387-3

Printed in the United States of America

2 3 4 5 6 7 8 9 RMN 20 19 18 17 16

B

# ELD
## Companion Worktext

**Program Authors**

Diane August

Jana Echevarria

Josefina V. Tinajero

McGraw Hill Education

# Unit 4

# Meet the Challenge

**The Big Idea**
What are the different ways to meet challenges?

# Unit 4

# Meet the Challenge

## The Big Idea

What are different ways to meet challenges?

**? Essential Question**

What choices are good for us?

>> *Go Digital*

**COLLABORATE** Look at the picture. What healthy choice did the girl make? Write healthy choices in the chart. Tell why the choices are healthy.

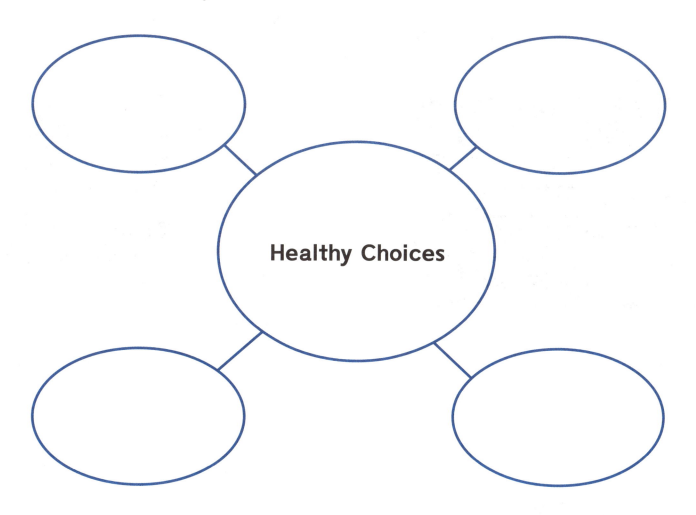

Healthy Choices

Discuss why some choices are healthy. Use the words from the chart. You can say:

Choose to _____ to feed your body vitamins.

Choose to _____ to stay in good shape.

Choose to _____ to do well in school.

# More Vocabulary

Look at the picture and read the word. Then read the sentences. Talk about the word with a partner. Write your own sentence.

**approached**

The bear **approached** the water.

What word means the opposite of *approach*?

**drink**          **see**          **leave**

**Why does the bear approach the water?**

The bear approaches the water _____

_____.

**contributions**

We made **contributions** to the food drive.

What word means almost the same as *contributions*?

**gifts**          **games**          **homes**

**What kinds of contributions do people give?**

People give contributions of _____

_____.

# Words and Phrases: Compound Words

**Compound Words**

A compound word is two short words that make one long word.

*farm + house* = farmhouse
What kind of house is on a farm?

A <u>farmhouse</u> is on a farm.

*black + bird* = blackbird

What kind of bird is in the tree?

A <u>blackbird</u> is in the tree.

**COLLABORATE** Talk with a partner. Look at the pictures. Read the sentences. Circle the compound word that means the same as the underlined words.

We made a <u>bath for birds</u>.
**birdbath**     **bluebird**

I have a <u>coat for the rain</u>.
**rainbow**     **raincoat**

(tl)Christian Lagereek/Photographer's Choice RF/Getty Images; (tr)Ziga Camernik/iStock/Getty Images Plus; (bl)AllegressePhotography/iStock/Getty Images Plus; (br)Martin Mark Soerensen/iStock/Getty Images Plus

**1 Talk About It**

Look at the picture. Read the title. Discuss what you see. Use these words.

**soup    nail    man
boy    walking**

Write about what you see.

What does the title tell you?

The story is about _____.

The soup is made from a _____.

What does the picture show?

The picture shows a _____

and _____.

They are _____

_____

_____.

Take notes as you read the story.

# Nail Soup

**Essential Question**

**What choices are good for us?**

Read about how choices helped a man and his wife learn a lesson.

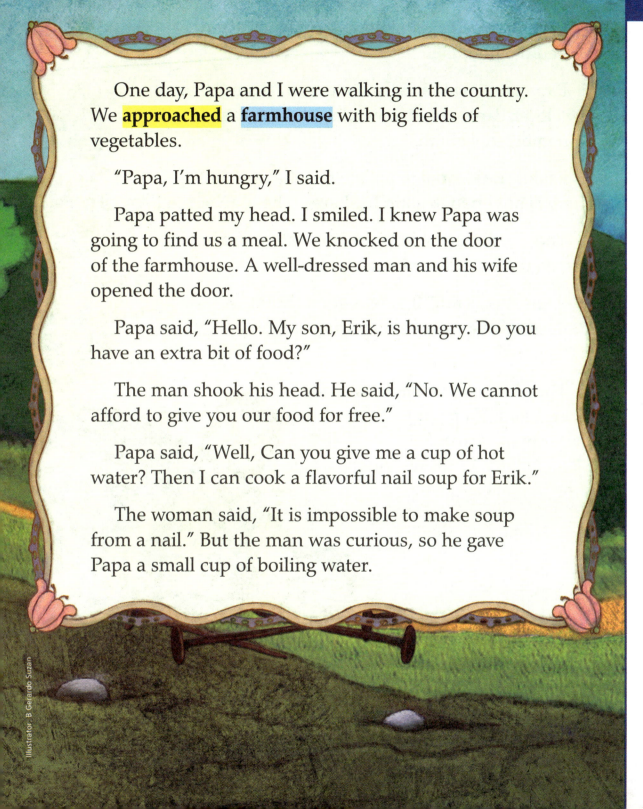

One day, Papa and I were walking in the country. We **approached** a **farmhouse** with big fields of vegetables.

"Papa, I'm hungry," I said.

Papa patted my head. I smiled. I knew Papa was going to find us a meal. We knocked on the door of the farmhouse. A well-dressed man and his wife opened the door.

Papa said, "Hello. My son, Erik, is hungry. Do you have an extra bit of food?"

The man shook his head. He said, "No. We cannot afford to give you our food for free."

Papa said, "Well, Can you give me a cup of hot water? Then I can cook a flavorful nail soup for Erik."

The woman said, "It is impossible to make soup from a nail." But the man was curious, so he gave Papa a small cup of boiling water.

Illustrator: B Gerardo Suzan

**1 Comprehension**
**Point of View**

Who is telling the story? Underline the words in the first sentence that tell you.

**2 Specific Vocabulary** A C T

Reread the second sentence. The word *farmhouse* means "a house on a farm." *Farmhouse* is made from two smaller words. Write the two words.

_____

_____

What is near the farmhouse? Draw a box around the words.

**3 Sentence Structure** A C T

Look at the fourth paragraph. Circle the quotation marks that show someone is speaking. Who is speaking? Write the word.

_____

9

# Text Evidence

## 1 Sentence Structure A C T

Reread the first sentence. An adjective is a word that describes a noun. Write the adjective in this sentence and the noun it describes.

The word _____

describes the _____.

## 2 Comprehension
### Point of View

Reread the second paragraph. What does the boy think about his Papa?

The boy thinks _____

_____.

## 3 Specific Vocabulary A C T

Look at the word *aromatic*. Something that is aromatic has a nice, strong smell. What will make the soup more *aromatic*? Underline the word that tells you.

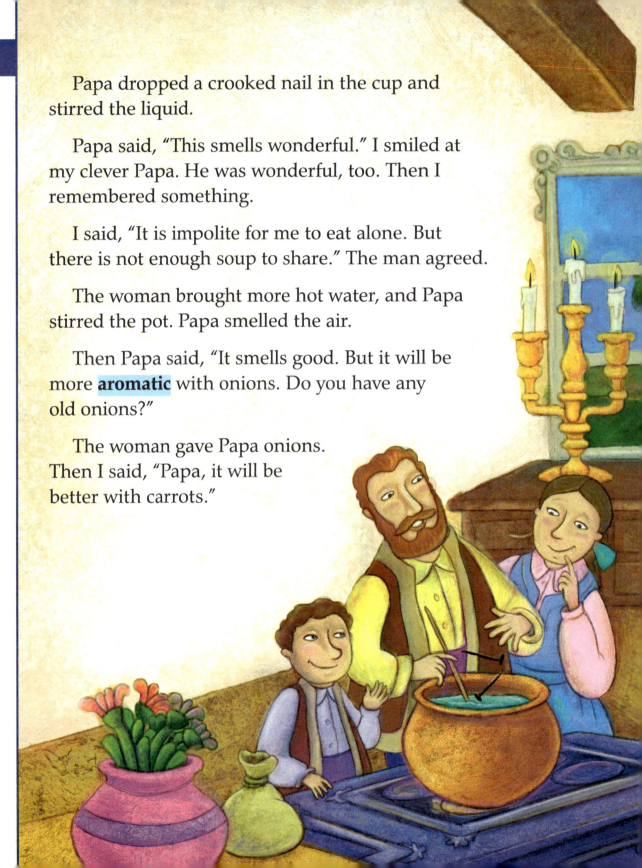

Papa dropped a crooked nail in the cup and stirred the liquid.

Papa said, "This smells wonderful." I smiled at my clever Papa. He was wonderful, too. Then I remembered something.

I said, "It is impolite for me to eat alone. But there is not enough soup to share." The man agreed.

The woman brought more hot water, and Papa stirred the pot. Papa smelled the air.

Then Papa said, "It smells good. But it will be more aromatic with onions. Do you have any old onions?"

The woman gave Papa onions. Then I said, "Papa, it will be better with carrots."

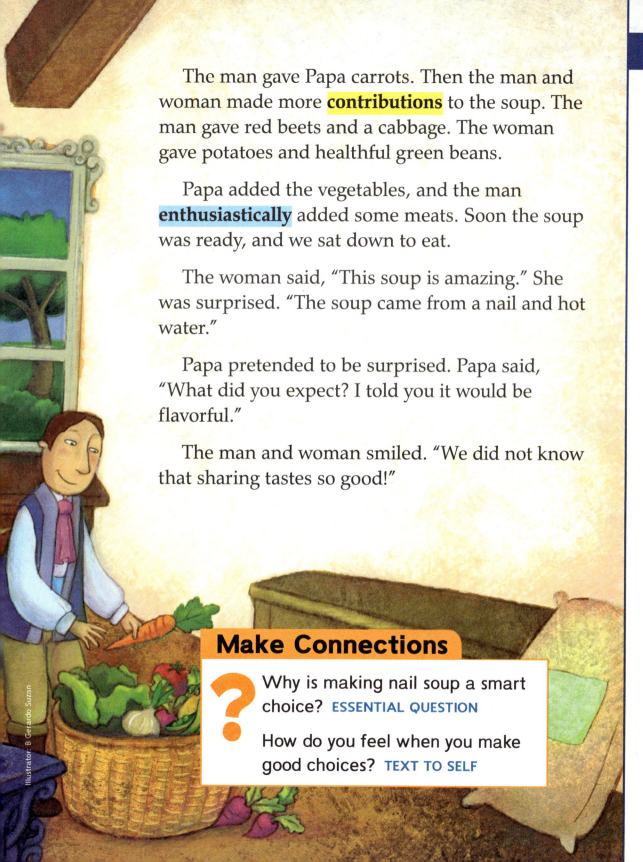

The man gave Papa carrots. Then the man and woman made more **contributions** to the soup. The man gave red beets and a cabbage. The woman gave potatoes and healthful green beans.

Papa added the vegetables, and the man **enthusiastically** added some meats. Soon the soup was ready, and we sat down to eat.

The woman said, "This soup is amazing." She was surprised. "The soup came from a nail and hot water."

Papa pretended to be surprised. Papa said, "What did you expect? I told you it would be flavorful."

The man and woman smiled. "We did not know that sharing tastes so good!"

## Make Connections

**?** Why is making nail soup a smart choice? ESSENTIAL QUESTION

How do you feel when you make good choices? TEXT TO SELF

Illustrator: B Gerardo Suzan

**1 Specific Vocabulary** Ⓐ Ⓒ Ⓣ

Look at the second paragraph. The word *enthusiastically* means "showing you are excited." What does the man do enthusiastically? Underline the words that tell you.

**2 Sentence Structure** Ⓐ Ⓒ Ⓣ

Reread the third paragraph. Circle the pronoun *she*. Who does the pronoun *she* refer to? Write the word.

_____

COLLABORATE

**3 Talk About It**

How do the man and woman feel about sharing by the end of the story? Justify your answer.

The man and woman feel _____.

The text says _____

_____

# Respond to the Text

**Partner Discussion** Work with a partner. Read the questions about "Nail Soup." Show where you found text evidence. Write the page numbers. Then discuss what you learned.

| How does Papa make nail soup? | **Text Evidence** 🔍 |
|---|---|
| First, Papa asks for _____. | Page(s): _____ |
| Then, Papa asks for _____. | Page(s): _____ |

| How do the man and woman feel about nail soup? | **Text Evidence** 🔍 |
|---|---|
| First, the woman thinks nail soup _____. | Page(s): _____ |
| Then the man and woman bring Papa _____. | Page(s): _____ |
| Then they eat _____ | Page(s): _____ |
| and say _____. | |

**Group Discussion** Present your answers to the group. Cite text evidence for your ideas. Listen to and discuss the group's opinions.

**Write** Work with a partner. Look at your notes about "Nail Soup." Write your answer to the Essential Question. Use text evidence to support your answer. Use vocabulary words in your writing.

**How does nail soup teach the man and woman a lesson?**

First, Papa asks for _____

so _____.

The man and woman think nail soup _____

but they _____.

When the soup is ready, the man and woman _____

_____.

Then they say _____.

**Share Writing** Present your writing to the class. Discuss their opinions. Talk about their ideas. Explain why you agree or disagree with their ideas. You can say:

I think your idea is _____.

I do not agree because _____.

# Write to Sources

pages 8–11

Lizzie

**Take Notes About the Text** I took notes on this chart to answer the question: *Do you think Papa's plan to make nail soup is a good idea? Use details from the story to support your answer.*

Papa asks the man and woman for food.

↓

The mean man and woman say no.

↓

Papa asks for a cup of hot water and puts a nail in it.

↓

Papa tricks the man and woman.

↓

The man and woman put vegetables in the water.

**Write About the Text** I used notes to write an opinion. I supported my opinion with facts from the story.

Papa's plan to make nail soup is a good idea. Papa asks a man and a woman for some food. The mean man and woman say no. So Papa asks for some hot water. He says he wants to make nail soup. Then Papa tricks the man and woman. They put vegetables in the soup. Papa's idea is good. He gets food for his son.

## TALK ABOUT IT

COLLABORATE

### Text Evidence

**Underline** the third sentence. Which word shows how Lizzie feels about the man and woman?

### Grammar

**Draw a box** around the sentence about Papa's plan. What is the linking verb in the sentence?

### Connect Ideas

**Circle** the last two sentences. How can you use the word *because* to connect the ideas?

COLLABORATE

### Your Turn

Do you think the man and woman make good choices? Use text evidence to support your answer.

**>> Go Digital**
Write your response online. Use your editing checklist.

15

# TALK ABOUT IT

**? Essential Question**

How can you use what you know to help others?

**>> Go Digital**

16

**COLLABORATE** What is the man's talent? How is the man helping others?
Write talents in the chart. Tell how you can use these talents.

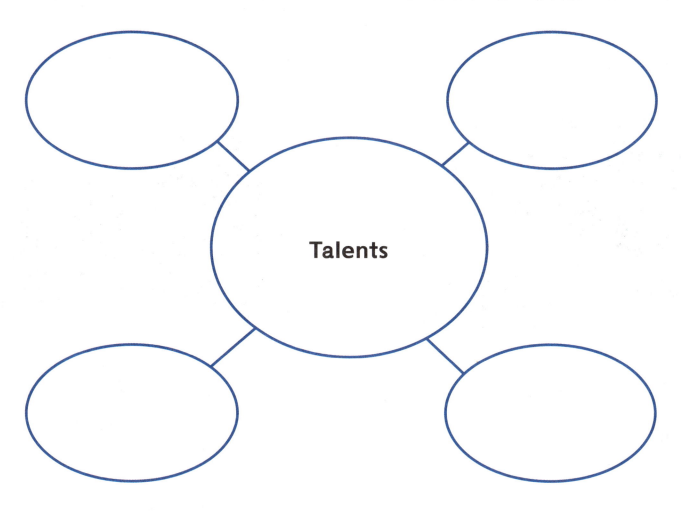

Talents

Tell how you can use talents to help others. Use the words from the chart. You can say:

You can use _____ to help others with school projects.

You can use _____ to help others laugh.

You can use _____ to help others with exercise.

# More Vocabulary

Look at the picture and read the word. Then read the sentences. Talk about the word with a partner. Write your own sentence.

**incredible**

The dog does an **incredible** trick.

What word means *incredible*?

smart          amazing          little

**What incredible things have you seen?**

I saw an incredible _____

_____.

**relaxed**

Anna feels **relaxed**.

What word means *relaxed*?

calm          sad          kind

**When do you feel relaxed?**

I feel relaxed when _____

_____.

18

(l)John Giustina/Getty Images; (r)Jose Luis Pelaez Inc/Getty Images

# Words and Phrases: Shades of Meaning: Synonyms

**The word *big* means "large."**

What size is the dog?

The dog is **big**.

**The word *gigantic* means "very, very large."**

How large is the whale?

The whale is **gigantic**.

**COLLABORATE**

**Talk with a partner. Look at the pictures. Read the sentences. Write the word that completes the sentence.**

The truck is _____.

        big     gigantic

The truck is _____.

        big     gigantic

**COLLABORATE**

## 1 Talk About It

Look at the picture. Read the title. Discuss what you see. Use these words.

**pet show     girl     boy large dog**

Write about what you see.

What does the title tell you?

This is a story about a _____

_____

_____.

What does the picture show?

The picture shows a _____,

a _____, and a

_____.

Take notes as you read the story.

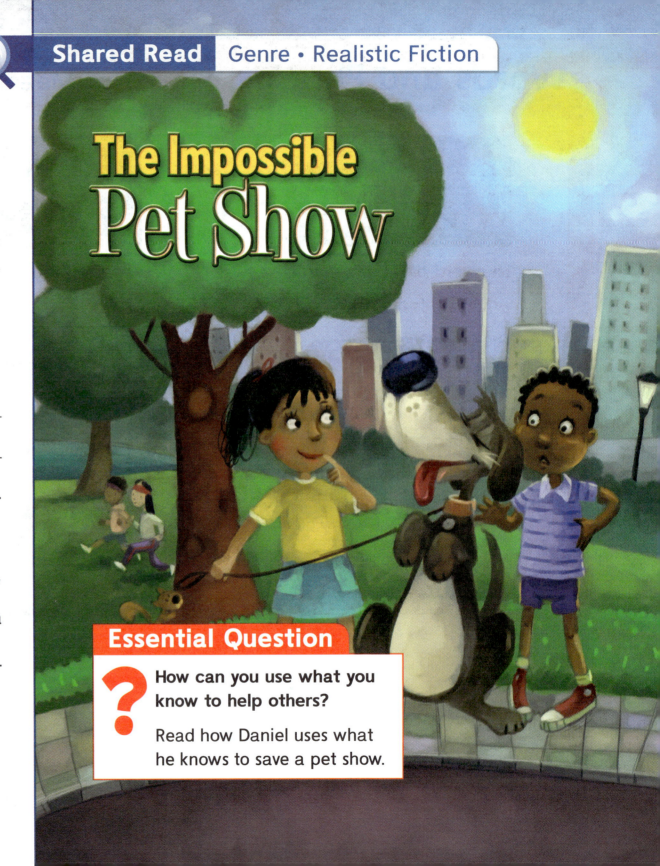

# The Impossible Pet Show

## Essential Question

**?** How can you use what you know to help others?

Read how Daniel uses what he knows to save a pet show.

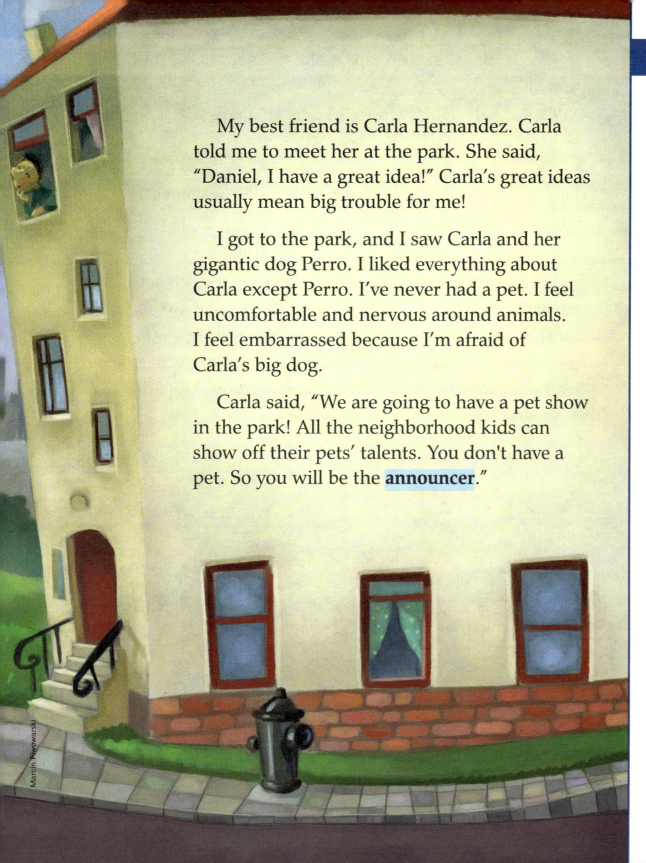

My best friend is Carla Hernandez. Carla told me to meet her at the park. She said, "Daniel, I have a great idea!" Carla's great ideas usually mean big trouble for me!

I got to the park, and I saw Carla and her gigantic dog Perro. I liked everything about Carla except Perro. I've never had a pet. I feel uncomfortable and nervous around animals. I feel embarrassed because I'm afraid of Carla's big dog.

Carla said, "We are going to have a pet show in the park! All the neighborhood kids can show off their pets' talents. You don't have a pet. So you will be the **announcer**."

Marcin Piwowarski

**1 Sentence Structure** **A C T**

Reread the first sentence of the second paragraph. Circle the word that breaks the sentence into two parts. Underline each part.

**2 Comprehension**
**Point of View**

Reread the second paragraph. How does Daniel feel about Perro? Underline the words that tell you.

**3 Specific Vocabulary** **A C T**

Look at the last sentence in the third paragraph. In this sentence, *announcer* means "the leader of a show or event." Who will be the announcer at the pet show?

## ❶ Comprehension
### Point of View

Reread the first paragraph. How does Daniel feel about crowds? Underline the sentence that tells you.

## ❷ Sentence Structure Ⓐ Ⓒ Ⓣ

Reread the second paragraph. Circle the punctuation marks that show someone is speaking. Then write the name of the speaker.

_____

## ❸ Specific Vocabulary Ⓐ Ⓒ Ⓣ

Look at the word *anxious*. An anxious person feels nervous and worried. Why is Daniel anxious? Draw a box around the words that tell you.

I said, "But Carla, crowds make me nervous. And I don't like pets."

Carla said, "Don't worry. I know that you will be great!"

Then, Perro leaped up and slobbered all over me. He almost knocked me down. "Down, Perro! Stay!" I shouted. Perro sat still as a statue.

"Wow, you're good at that," said Carla.

On Saturday morning, people came to see the pet show. The crowd was big, and it made me feel **anxious**.

Then the show started, and I announced the first pet. It was a parakeet named Butter. His talent was walking back and forth on a wire. Everyone clapped and cheered, and I felt more **relaxed**.

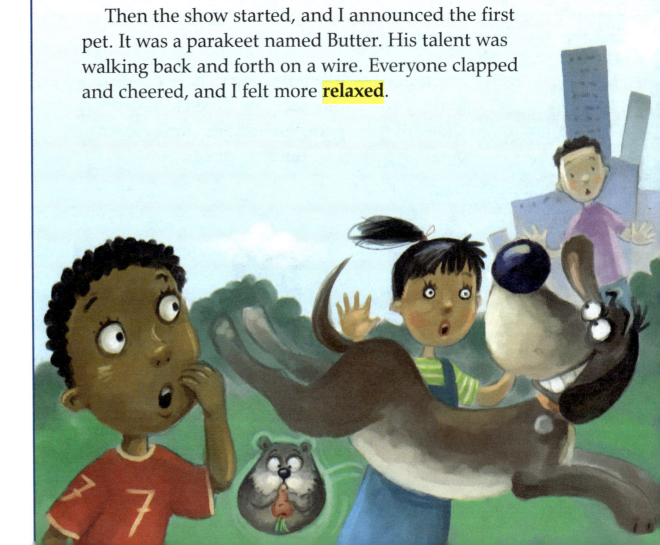

Then it was Carla and Perro's turn.

"Sit, Perro," she said. Perro didn't sit. Perro wasn't paying attention to Carla. He was watching Jack's bunnies jump around. Then Perro leaped at the bunnies. The bunnies hopped away and knocked over the hamster's cage. Pudgy, the hamster, escaped. Kyle's dog, Jake, howled. This show was a disaster, and I had to do something.

"Sit!" I shouted at Perro. "Quiet!" I ordered Jake.

"Stay!" I yelled. The animals and people all stopped and stared at me.

"Daniel, that was ==incredible=," said Carla. "You got the pets to **settle down**!"

Sadly, that was the end of our pet show. But now I have more confidence when I speak in front of people. Now Perro and I are great friends. And I have discovered my talent, too.

Marcin Piwowarski

## Make Connections

How does Daniel use what he knows to help others? **ESSENTIAL QUESTION**

Discuss if you want to be part of a pet show. **TEXT TO SELF**

**1 Sentence Structure** Ⓐ Ⓒ Ⓣ

Reread the last sentence in the second paragraph. Circle the word *and*. It connects the two clauses. Why does Daniel have to do something? Draw a box around the clause that tells you.

**2 Specific Vocabulary** Ⓐ Ⓒ Ⓣ

The idiom *settle down* in the fifth paragraph means "relax" or "be calm." How does Daniel get the pets to settle down? Underline the words in the third and fourth paragraphs.

COLLABORATE

**3 Talk About It**

How does Daniel change at the end of the story?

Daniel says that he and Perro

_____.

Daniel discovers _____.

23

# Respond to the Text

**Partner Discussion** Work with a partner. Read the questions about "The Impossible Pet Show." Show where you found text evidence. Write the page numbers. Then discuss what you learned.

---

**What happens at the pet show?**

First, Perro leaps at _____.

Next, the bunnies knock over _____.

Then the hamster escapes and _____.

**Text Evidence**

Page(s): _____

Page(s): _____

Page(s): _____

---

**What does Daniel do at the pet show?**

First, Daniel shouts at _____.

Next Daniel tells _____.

Finally, Daniel yells ____ and everyone _____.

**Text Evidence**

Page(s): _____

Page(s): _____

Page(s): _____

---

**Group Discussion** Present your answers to the group. Cite text evidence for your ideas. Listen to and discuss the group's opinions.

**Write** Work with a partner. Look at your notes about "The Impossible Pet Show." Write your answer to the Essential Question. Use text evidence to support your answer. Use vocabulary words in your writing.

**What does Daniel do to save the pet show?**

Perro leaps at the _____

and the hamster _____.

Daniel decides to _____.

So Daniel shouts at _____ and orders Jake to _____

_____.

Daniel saves the show because he can make pets _____

_____.

**Share Writing** Present your writing to the class. Discuss their opinions. Talk about their ideas. Explain why you agree or disagree with their ideas. You can say:

I agree with _____.

That's a good comment, but _____.

# Write to Sources

pages 20–23

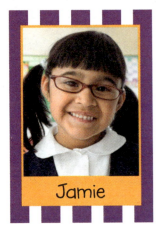

Jamie

**Take Notes About the Text** I took notes on this chart to answer the question: *Do you think Daniel is a good announcer for the pet show?*

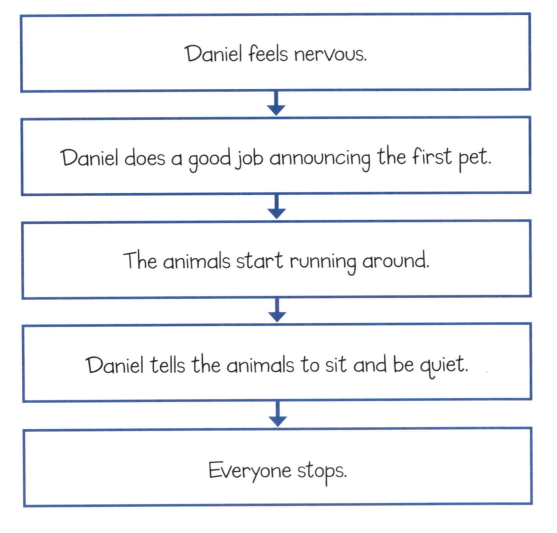

Daniel feels nervous.

↓

Daniel does a good job announcing the first pet.

↓

The animals start running around.

↓

Daniel tells the animals to sit and be quiet.

↓

Everyone stops.

**Write About the Text** I used notes from my chart to write an opinion. I used details from the story to support my opinion.

**Student Model:** *Opinion*

I think Daniel is a good announcer for the pet show. Daniel is very nervous. But he does a good job announcing the first pet. Then the animals start running around. Daniel tells them to sit and be quiet. Everyone stops. That is why Daniel is a good announcer for the pet show.

COLLABORATE

**TALK ABOUT IT**

**Text Evidence**
**Underline** the fifth sentence. Does this sentence help support Jamie's opinion?

**Grammar**
**Draw a box** around the sentence that tells how Daniel feels. How can you add the words *at first* to show when Daniel is nervous?

**Connect Ideas**
**Circle** the fourth and fifth sentences. Use the the word *so* to connect the ideas.

COLLABORATE

**Your Turn**

Would you be a good announcer for a pet show? Tell why or why not.

>> *Go Digital*
Write your response online. Use your editing checklist.

**?** **Essential Question**

How do animals adapt to challenges in their habitat?

» *Go Digital*

How does the ermine hide in the snow? In the chart, write other ways that animals change. Discuss how different habitats affect animals.

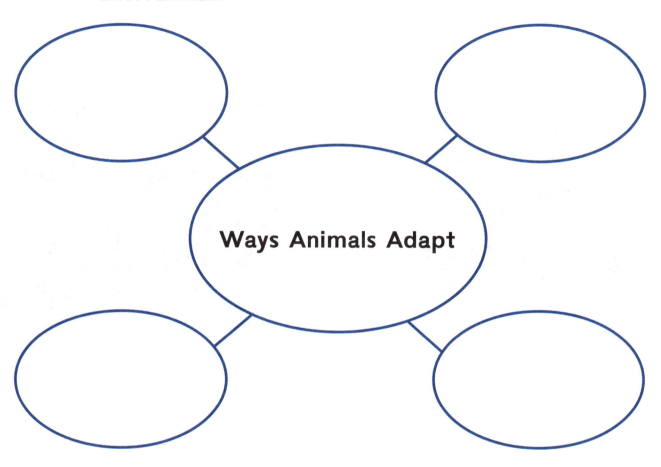

Ways Animals Adapt

Discuss how adaptations help animals to survive. Use the words from the chart. You can say:

Animals can change _____ to help them _____.

Animals have different kinds of _____ to chew food.

Animals grow or lose their _____ in hot or cold weather.

Animals move at faster _____ to get away from danger.

# More Vocabulary

Look at the picture and read the word. Then read the sentences. Talk about the word with a partner. Write your own sentence.

**adapted**

Polar bears **adapted** to the snow and cold.

Complete the sentence. Write the word.

I adapt to cold days by _____

**How do polar bears adapt to cold days?**

Polar bears adapt by _____

_____.

**danger**

Fire is a **danger** to trees.

Complete the sentence. Write the word.

Fire is also a danger to _____.

**What are some other dangers?**

_____

_____ are dangers.

# Words and Phrases: Multiple-Meaning Words

*pack* = a group of wild animals

What animals live in a pack?

Hyenas live in a `pack`.

*pack* = to put things in a box, case, bag, or car

What do Dad and Roy pack?

They `pack` the car.

**COLLABORATE** Talk with a partner. Look at the pictures. Read the sentences. Circle the meaning of the underlined word.

The <u>pack</u> of wolves lives in the woods.

**group of wild animals**       **put things in a box, case, or bag**

Mom <u>packs</u> Ivy's lunch every day.

**group of wild animals**       **put things in a box, case, or bag**

COLLABORATE

## 1 Talk About It

Look at the picture. Read the title. Discuss what you see. Use these words.

**wolf    fox    gray    red    fur**

Write about what you see.

What animals are in the picture?

The picture shows _____

_____

_____.

How are the animals alike?

Describe what you see.

_____

_____

**Take notes as you read the text.**

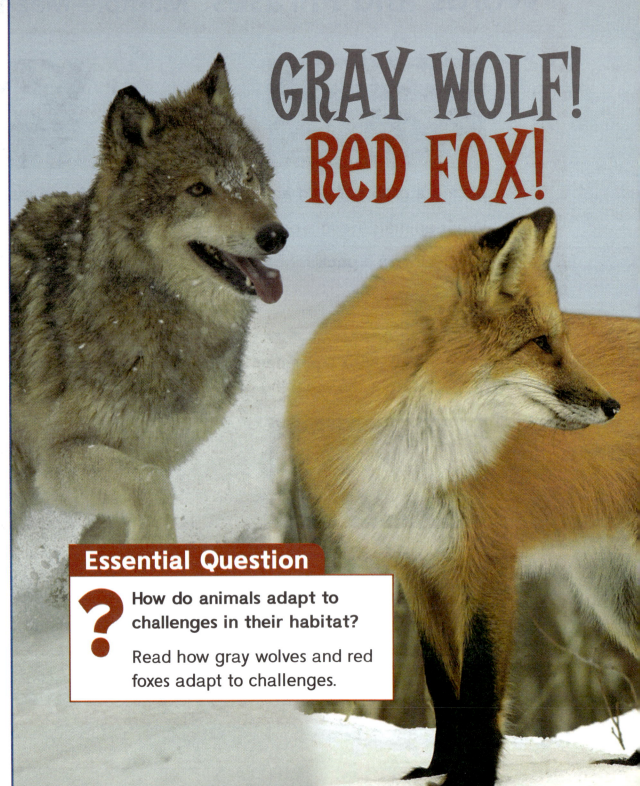

# GRAY WOLF!
# RED FOX!

## Essential Question

**?** **How do animals adapt to challenges in their habitat?**

Read how gray wolves and red foxes adapt to challenges.

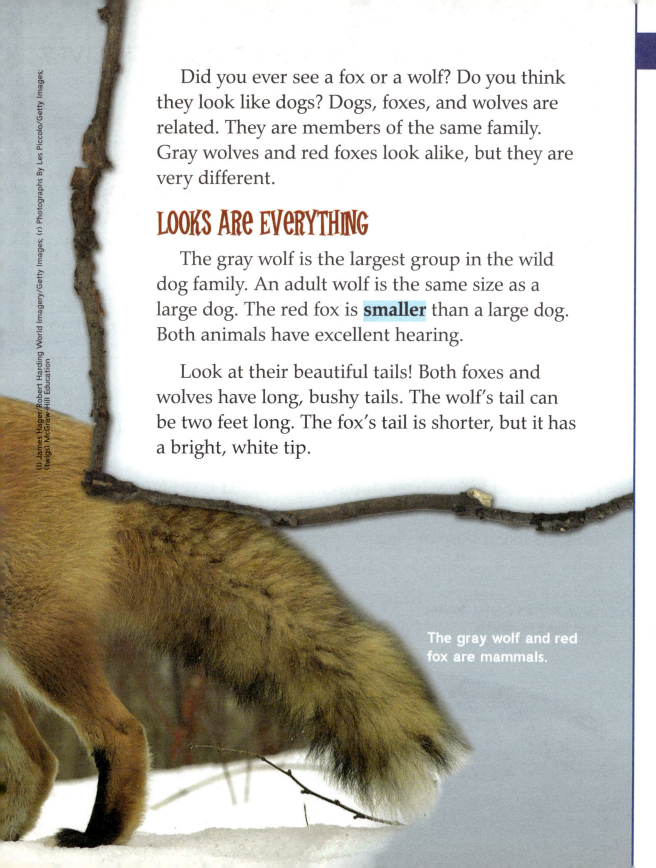

Did you ever see a fox or a wolf? Do you think they look like dogs? Dogs, foxes, and wolves are related. They are members of the same family. Gray wolves and red foxes look alike, but they are very different.

## LOOKS ARE EVERYTHING

The gray wolf is the largest group in the wild dog family. An adult wolf is the same size as a large dog. The red fox is **smaller** than a large dog. Both animals have excellent hearing.

Look at their beautiful tails! Both foxes and wolves have long, bushy tails. The wolf's tail can be two feet long. The fox's tail is shorter, but it has a bright, white tip.

The gray wolf and red fox are mammals.

### ① Comprehension
### Compare and Contrast

Look at the last sentence in the first paragraph. What two animals are being compared?

_____

### ② Specific Vocabulary ACT

Look at the adjective *smaller* in the second paragraph. The suffix *-er* at the end of the word *small* means "more." What does the word *smaller* mean?

_____

Which animal is smaller than a large dog? Circle the noun.

### ③ Sentence Structure ACT

Reread the last sentence in the third paragraph. What adjectives describe the noun *tip*? Underline the adjectives.

# Text Evidence

### 1 Specific Vocabulary ACT

Look at the adjective *thick*. The word *thick* means "has a lot of something." What is thick? Circle the word.

### 2 Sentence Structure ACT

Reread sentence two in the second paragraph. The word *because* connects the two parts of the sentence. Underline the part that tells what people caused.

### 3 Comprehension
### Compare and Contrast

Reread the last paragraph. What foods do red foxes and wolves eat?

Red foxes eat _____

_____.

Wolves eat _____

_____.

Foxes and wolves have **thick** fur to keep them warm. Their coats can be white, brown, or black. Red foxes have red fur. But a gray wolf's fur is more gray than brown.

## FINDING FOOD

Gray wolves and red foxes live in many different habitats. Both animals lost their homes because of people. The red fox has **adapted** well to fit into its environment. Now many foxes make their homes near towns. But wolves stay far away from people.

Foxes and wolves have different diets. Red foxes hunt alone. They eat small animals, birds, and fish. Wolves eat large animals like moose or deer.

**WHERE DO THEY LIVE?**

United States of America

N W E S

**LEGEND**
- Red Fox only
- Gray Wolf only
- Both

**Gray wolves prefer to live and hunt in packs.**

## DAY-TO-DAY

Wolves live in packs, or groups, of four to seven. They hunt and **travel** together. They sleep in dens for shelter. Foxes like to live alone. They sleep in fields or empty holes.

Both wolves and foxes communicate by barking and growling. Gray wolves howl to alert, or warn, other wolves of **danger**. Red foxes wave their tails to warn other foxes.

The gray wolf and red fox have many things in common. But they are very different animals.

The red fox hunts for food alone.

### Make Connections

**?** How did the gray wolf and the red fox adapt? **ESSENTIAL QUESTION**

Which animal would you like to learn more about? Why? **TEXT TO SELF**

(tl) Mapping Specialists, Ltd., Madison, WI; (b) Corbis Bridge/Alamy; (tr) jimkruger/iStock/360/Getty Images; (twigs) McGraw-Hill Education

---

## Text Evidence

**1 Specific Vocabulary** A C T

The word *travel* means "to go from one place to another." Circle the word that tells how wolves travel.

**2 Comprehension**

**Compare and Contrast**

Reread the second paragraph. Which detail shows how a red fox is different from a gray wolf? Underline the detail.

**COLLABORATE**

**3 Talk About It**

How are gray wolves and red foxes the same? Write your ideas. Use text evidence.

Gray wolves and red foxes both

_____

_____

_____

# Respond to the Text

**Partner Discussion** Work with a partner. Read the questions about "Gray Wolf! Red Fox!" Show where you found text evidence. Write the page numbers. Then discuss what you learned.

**How have red foxes adapted?**

Red foxes have excellent _____.

Red foxes like to live _____.

Red foxes have thick fur to _____.

**Text Evidence**

Page(s): _____

Page(s): _____

Page(s): _____

**How have gray wolves adapted?**

Gray wolves have excellent _____.

Gray wolves do almost everything _____.

Gray wolves have thick fur to _____.

**Text Evidence**

Page(s): _____

Page(s): _____

Page(s): _____

**Group Discussion** Present your answers to the group. Cite text evidence for your ideas. Listen to and discuss the group's opinions.

**Write** Work with a partner. Look at your notes about "Gray Wolf! Red Fox!" Write your answer to the Essential Question. Use text evidence to support your answer. Use vocabulary words in your writing.

How have gray wolves and red foxes adapted to challenges?

Both red foxes and gray wolves have excellent _____.

Gray wolves hunt in packs because _____.

Red foxes live _____.

Both gray wolves and red foxes have _____.

Both red foxes and gray wolves _____.

**Share Writing** Present your writing to the class. Discuss their opinions. Talk about their ideas. Explain why you agree or disagree with their ideas. You can say:

I think your idea is _____.

I do not agree because _____.

# Write to Sources

Luke

**Take Notes About the Text** I took notes about the text on this chart to answer the questions: *How are red foxes and gray wolves the same? How are they different? Use details from the text in your answer.*

pages 32–35

| How They Hunt | What They Eat |
|---|---|
| Red foxes hunt alone. | Red foxes eat small animals. |
| Gray wolves hunt in groups. | Gray wolves eat large animals. |

**Write About the Text** I used notes from my chart to write an informative paragraph about foxes and wolves.

## Student Model: *Informative Text*

How do red foxes and gray wolves hunt? They hunt in different ways. Red foxes hunt alone, but gray wolves hunt in groups. What do red foxes and gray wolves eat? Red foxes eat animals. Gray wolves eat animals. Gray wolves eat large animals. Red foxes eat small animals. Red foxes and gray wolves are the same in some ways, but they are also different.

**TALK ABOUT IT**

### Text Evidence
**Circle** the second sentence. What evidence does Luke use to support this statement?

### Grammar
**Underline** the second sentence. **Draw a box** around the subject of the sentence. What does the pronoun *they* refer to this sentence?

### Condense Ideas
**Circle** the fifth and sixth sentences. How can you condense the sentences?

**Your Turn**

Do red foxes and gray wolves look the same or different? Use details from the text in your response.

**>> Go Digital**
Write your response online. Use your editing checklist.

# TALK ABOUT IT

## Weekly Concept Flight

**? Essential Question**

How are people able to fly?

>> *Go Digital*

COLLABORATE

**Look at the picture. How is the person flying? Write words about flight in the chart. Tell how people fly.**

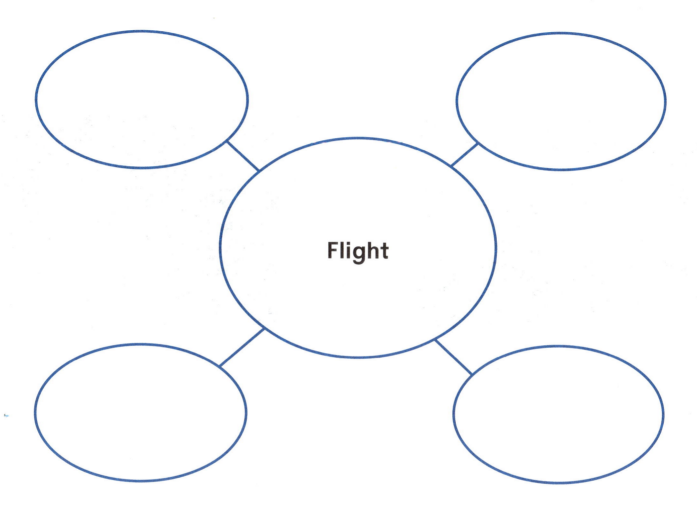

Flight

**Tell how people learned to fly. Use the words from the chart. You can say:**

People studied a _____ wings to learn about flying.

Inventors designed planes that had _____.

The planes could fly people into the _____.

Look at the picture and read the word. Then read the sentences. Talk about the word with a partner. Write your own sentence.

**machine**

A car is a <mark>machine</mark>.

Complete the sentence. Write the word.

A computer is a _____.

**What <mark>machines</mark> do you use?**

Some machines that I use are _____

_____.

**unlocked**

I <mark>unlocked</mark> the answer to the math problem.

What word means the same as *unlocked*?

checked        solved        called

**What problems have you <mark>unlocked</mark>?**

I have unlocked _____

_____.

# Words and Phrases: Comparative Suffixes

*tall* + *-er* = more tall

Who is tall**er**?

The boy is **taller**.

*tall* + *-est* = most tall

Who is the tall**est**?

Dad is the **tallest**.

**COLLABORATE** Talk with a partner. Look at the pictures. Read the sentences. Write the word that completes the sentence.

The dog is _____ than the kitten.

**bigger**  **biggest**

The _____ person in the photo is my Grandpa.

**older**  **oldest**

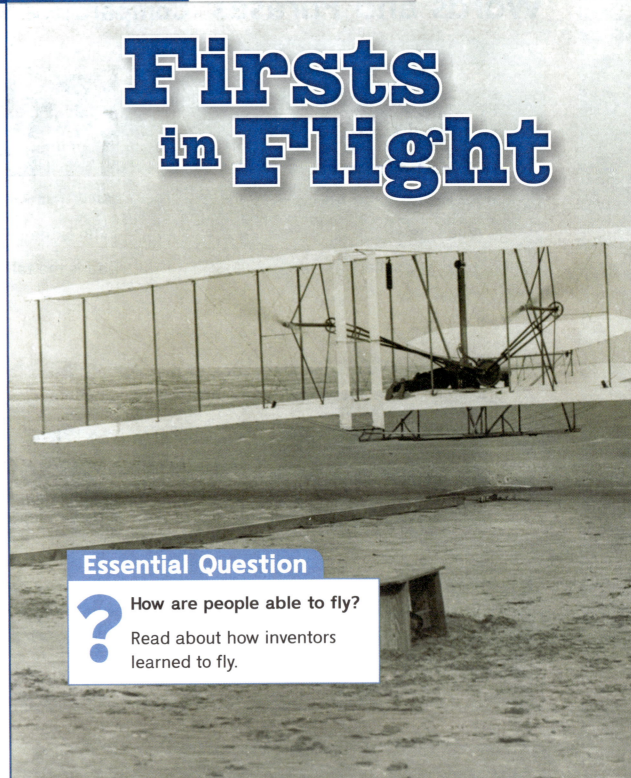

# Firsts in Flight

**1 Talk About It**

Look at the picture. Read the title. Discuss what you see. Use these words.

**airplane    inventors    history**

What does the title tell you?

This is a text about _____

_____.

What does the photograph show?

The photograph shows _____

_____

_____.

Take notes as you read the text.

**Essential Question**

**?** **How are people able to fly?**

Read about how inventors learned to fly.

Orville and Wilbur Wright

The Wright brothers owned a bicycle shop in Ohio. But their **dream** was to fly. They built flying **machines**, and they flew the first one in 1899. But the winds in Ohio were not strong enough to keep the machine in motion.

The brothers needed a place where the winds were stronger. So the Wright brothers chose Kitty Hawk, North Carolina to test their newest flying machine. It was windy there. Also, the sandy beaches made their landings softer.

On December 17, 1903, the Wright Flyer flew at Kitty Hawk.

(bkgd)Transtock/SuperStock; (inset)Everett Collection/SuperStock

# Text Evidence

**1 Specific Vocabulary** A C T

Look at the word *dream*. The word *dream* means "a wish to do something." Underline the words that tell what the Wright brothers' dream was.

**2 Sentence Structure** A C T

Reread the third sentence. Circle the comma and the word *and* in the middle of the sentence. The comma and the word *and* combine two shorter sentences. Draw a box around both of the two shorter sentences.

**3 Comprehension**
**Cause and Effect**

Why did the Wright brothers test their flying machine in Kitty Hawk? Use text evidence.

Kitty Hawk was _____

_____.

Kitty Hawk had _____

_____.

## ❶ Comprehension

### Cause and Effect

Look at the first paragraph. Why did the brothers learn a lot about flying?

The brothers learned a lot about

flying because _____

_____ .

## ❷ Specific Vocabulary Ⓐ Ⓒ Ⓣ

*Gravity* is a science word. It describes why objects fall to the ground. Which words tell what happened when the brothers conquered gravity? Circle the words.

## ❸ Sentence Structure Ⓐ Ⓒ Ⓣ

Look at the last paragraph. Draw a box around the part of the third sentence that tells when other people tried to fly airplanes. Circle the punctuation that sets this information apart.

The Wright brothers' first flight was not successful. As a result, they learned a lot about flying. So they built a glider with bigger wings in 1900. It did not work well either. In 1903, they built the *Wright Flyer*. It was their first airplane with an engine.

## Flying Firsts

The Wright brothers were ready to test the *Wright Flyer*. Orville flew the plane. Wilbur watched from the ground. The flight lasted twelve seconds. With this flight, the Wright brothers conquered **gravity**. The plane moved in an upward direction. The brothers **unlocked** the secrets of flying.

Alberto Santos-Dumont was the third man in the world to fly a plane with an engine.

Heritage Images/Corbis

Orville and Wilbur continued to make better planes. Their flights became longer. Soon, other people tried to fly airplanes.

## Will It Fly?

Do an experiment on flying. Use a paper airplane.

**Materials needed:**

• pencil  • paper  • ruler

**Directions:**

1. Fold two paper airplanes with a partner. Make the planes' wings different.

2. Gently throw one plane.

3. Measure how far the plane flew. Write it down.

4. Throw the plane four more times. Take turns. Measure and write down how far it flies each time.

5. Do the same thing with the other airplane.

6. Compare how far each plane flew. Then talk about what you learned.

Alberto Santos-Dumont was an inventor and pilot from Brazil. In 1906, he made the first official flight in front of an audience. The next year, a French pilot flew with a passenger in his plane. They flew for one minute and fourteen seconds.

## Better Flying Machines

As time passed, better planes traveled longer distances. In 1909, a pilot flew across the English Channel.

Soon, inventors were building airplanes that carried more people. By 1920, new companies offered passengers the **chance** to fly. Humans had figured out how to fly!

This is what an airplane looked like in 1930.

### Make Connections

 How did the Wright brothers help people fly? **ESSENTIAL QUESTION**

Tell what you know about airplanes. Discuss other ways to fly. **TEXT TO SELF**

## Text Evidence

**1 Comprehension**
**Cause and Effect**

Look at the second paragraph. What happened when people invented better planes?

Better planes were able to

_____

**2 Specific Vocabulary** A C T

Reread the second sentence in the last paragraph. The word *chance* means something that is possible. Circle what passengers had the chance to do.

COLLABORATE

**3 Talk About It**

How did inventors make it possible for people to fly in airplanes? Cite text evidence.

Inventors made _____

_____.

47

# Respond to the Text

**COLLABORATE**

**Partner Discussion** Work with a partner. Read the questions about "Firsts in Flight." Show where you found text evidence. Write the page numbers. Then discuss what you learned.

**How did the Wright brothers learn to fly?**

The Wright brothers went to _____ to fly _____.

First, they flew gliders that _____.

They flew an airplane with an engine _____.

**Text Evidence** 🔍

Page(s): _____

Page(s): _____

Page(s): _____

**How did other inventors make flying possible?**

Alberto Santos-Dumont flew in front of _____.

Henri Farman flew with a _____.

Other inventors made planes that _____ and _____.

**Text Evidence** 🔍

Page(s): _____

Page(s): _____

Page(s): _____

**COLLABORATE**

**Group Discussion** Present your answers to the group. Cite text evidence for your ideas. Listen to and discuss the group's opinions.

**Write** Work with a partner. Look at your notes about "Firsts in Flight." Write your answer to the Essential Question. Use text evidence to support your answer. Use vocabulary words in your writing.

**How did inventors learn to fly?**

First, the Wright brothers flew _____

_____.

Then the Wright brothers made an airplane _____

_____.

Other inventors made _____ that flew _____ and

_____.

**Share Writing** Present your writing to the class. Discuss their opinions. Talk about their ideas. Explain why you agree or disagree with their ideas. You can say:

I agree with _____.

That's a good comment, but _____.

# Write to Sources

pages 44–47

Mina

**Take Notes About the Text** I took notes on this chart to answer the question: *How did the Wright brothers help people fly? Support your answer with text evidence.*

### Main Idea
The Wright brothers helped people fly because they built an airplane.

### Detail
The first flying machines did not work.

### Detail
The brothers tried to make a flying machine again.

### Detail
The brothers built an airplane in 1903.

### Detail
It flew for 12 seconds.

**Write About the Text** I used my notes to write about how the Wright brothers helped people fly.

## Student Model: *Informative Text*

The Wright brothers helped people fly because they built an airplane. The brothers made flying machines. The first machines did not work. The brothers tried again. Then the brothers built a plane in 1903. It flew for 12 seconds. Then other people started making airplanes. The Wright brothers' airplane helped people fly.

## TALK ABOUT IT

### Text Evidence
**Draw a box** around the conclusion. Does this sentence retell Mina's main idea in different words?

### Grammar
**Underline** the fifth sentence about when the Wright brothers built a plane. How can you add the words *with an engine* to describe the plane?

### Connect Ideas
**Circle** the third and fourth sentences. How can you use the word *so* to connect the ideas?

### Your Turn
Explain why it is important to try again when an invention does not work. Use text evidence to support your answer.

>> *Go Digital*
Write your response online. Use your editing checklist.

# TALK ABOUT IT

**?** **Essential Question**
How can others
inspire us?

>> *Go Digital*

**COLLABORATE**

**How does the fireman inspire others? Write words for people who inspire others in the chart. Talk about who inspires you.**

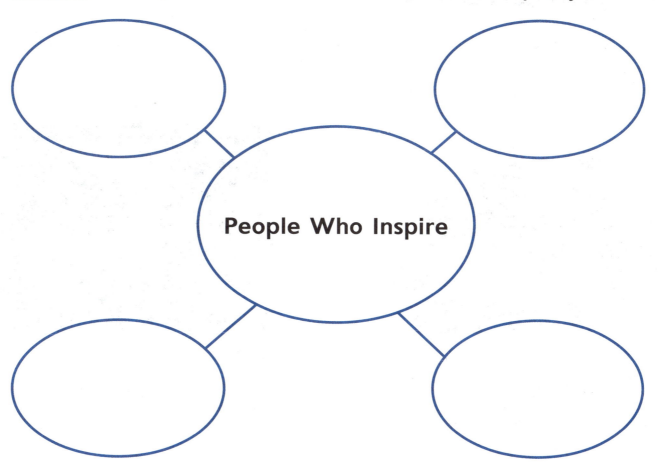

**People Who Inspire**

**Talk about people who inspire others. Use the words from the chart. You can say:**

A _____ and _____ can inspire

their children by working hard.

A _____ can inspire others by being a good leader.

A _____ can inspire others by being kind or helpful.

# More Vocabulary

 **Look at the picture. Read the word. Then read the sentences. Talk about the word with a partner. Answer the questions.**

**guide**

We used a map to **guide** us.

**What does the word *guide* mean?**

The word *guide* means _____

_____.

**pale**

The flowers are **pale** pink.

**What word means the opposite of *pale*?**

The opposite of *pale* is _____

_____.

(l)Radius Images/Alamy; (r)Svetlana Larina/Getty Images

# Poetry Terms

### metaphor

A **metaphor** compares two things. The two things are very different.

Our **ship** was a **bird**.

**ship = bird**

### rhyme

The words *cat* and *hat* **rhyme**. They end in the same sound.

The big black **cat** is asleep on my **hat**.

### repetition

**Repetition** repeats the same word or phrase.

I won! I won!

**COLLABORATE**

Work with a partner. Make up a rhyme. Use the words below. Say it together.

**hog   jog   dog**

The _____ likes

to _____ with

the _____.

(tl)Giovanni Rinaldi/iStock/Getty Images Plus; (tr)Don Hammond/Design Pics; (tr)Ariel Skelley/Blend Images LLC; (bl)Ingram Publishing; (br)Iconotec/Glow Images

**COLLABORATE**

## ❶ Talk About It

What is the poem about? How do you know? Discuss your answers. Write your ideas.

_____

_____

## ❷ Literary Element Repetition

Reread the first four lines of the poem. Circle the phrases that are repeated.

## ❸ Specific Vocabulary A C T

Look at the third section. Circle the word _terrified. Terrified_ means "really scared." Why was the crew terrified? Underline two details that tell you.

# Captain's Log,
## May 12, 1868

We set sail from a port in Spain,
Sun high, no sign of rain.
The sea was satin, so blue—so blue.
Our ship was a bird, we flew—we flew.

Just past noon, how very weird,
Came a sound that we most feared.
Thunder rumbled, a giant drum.
Thunder rumbled, rum tum tum.

Rain was pouring, pouring.
The wind was a monster, roaring, roaring.
My crew, extremely terrified,
Froze at their posts, pale and wide-eyed.

## Essential Question

**How can others inspire us?**

Read about different ways that people inspire others.

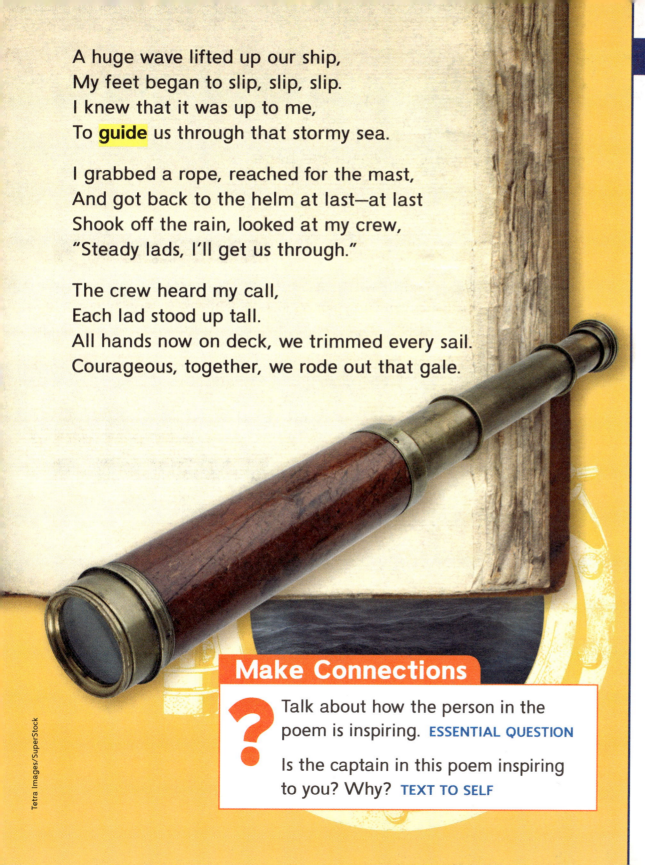

A huge wave lifted up our ship,
My feet began to slip, slip, slip.
I knew that it was up to me,
To **guide** us through that stormy sea.

I grabbed a rope, reached for the mast,
And got back to the helm at last—at last
Shook off the rain, looked at my crew,
"Steady lads, I'll get us through."

The crew heard my call,
Each lad stood up tall.
All hands now on deck, we trimmed every sail.
Courageous, together, we rode out that gale.

## Make Connections

**?** Talk about how the person in the poem is inspiring. **ESSENTIAL QUESTION**

Is the captain in this poem inspiring to you? Why? **TEXT TO SELF**

# Text Evidence

**1 Literary Element**
**Rhyme**

Reread the first section. Look at the third and fourth lines. Circle the words that rhyme. Write the words.

_____

_____

**2 Comprehension**
**Theme**

Reread the last section. Draw a box around the lines that show how the captain inspired the crew.

**COLLABORATE**

**3 Talk About It**

How does the captain describe the actions of the crew? Discuss your answer. Find the word that tells you. Write the word.

_____

# Respond to the Text

COLLABORATE

**Partner Discussion** Work with a partner. Read the questions about "Captain's Log." Show where you found text evidence. Write the page numbers. Then discuss what you learned.

---

**Why is the crew in danger?**

At first, the weather is _____.

Then rain begins _____.

A huge wave _____.

**Text Evidence** 🔍

Page(s): _____

Page(s): _____

Page(s): _____

---

**What does the captain do?**

First, the captain grabs _____.

Then the captain says _____.

The crew hear his call and _____.

**Text Evidence** 🔍

Page(s): _____

Page(s): _____

Page(s): _____

---

COLLABORATE

**Group Discussion** Present your answers to the group. Cite text evidence for your ideas. Listen to and discuss the group's opinions.

**Write** Work with a partner. Look at your notes about "Captain's Log." Write your answer to the Essential Question. Use text evidence to support your answer. Use vocabulary words in your writing.

**How does the captain inspire his crew?**

The crew feels terrified because _____.

A huge wave _____.

Then the captain grabs _____ and tells

the crew _____.

The captain and the crew _____

_____.

**Share Writing** Present your writing to the class. Discuss their opinions. Talk about their ideas. Explain why you agree or disagree with their ideas. You can say:

I agree with _____.

That's a good comment, but _____.

# Write to Sources

Juan

pages 56–57

**Take Notes About the Text** I took notes on this idea web to respond to the prompt: *Think about the metaphor "Our ship was a bird." Why does the poet use this metaphor in "Captain's Log"?*

The metaphor compares a ship and a bird.

Metaphor:
Our ship was a bird

A bird flies fast.

The ship moves fast in the water.

**Write About the Text** I used notes from my idea web to write a paragraph about the metaphor.

## Student Model: *Informative Text*

The poet uses the metaphor "our ship was a bird" in the poem. This metaphor helps readers picture the ship. The metaphor compares a ship and a bird. A bird flies fast. The poet means that the ship is fast. The metaphor helps me picture the ship. I can see it move fast in the water. The metaphor helps me see the ship in the poem.

## TALK ABOUT IT

### Text Evidence
**Underline** the third sentence. Which two sentences explain why the ship is like a bird?

### Grammar
**Draw a box** around the verb in the third sentence. Is this an action verb?

### Connect Ideas
**Underline** the fifth and sixth sentences. How can you use the connecting word *and* to combine these sentences?

## Your Turn

Describe another metaphor in "Captain's Log." Use details from the poem to explain your answer.

**>> Go Digital**
Write your response online. Use your editing checklist.

61